COLOR
YOURSELF CALM
POSTCARDS
50 PEACEFUL PASSAGES
TO COLOR AND SHARE

Thunder Bay Press
An imprint of Printers Row Publishing Group
10350 Barnes Canyon Road, Suite 100, San Diego, CA 92121
www.thunderbaybooks.com

Published in the French language originally under the title:
50 messages – pensées sereines à colorier et à envoyer
© 2014, Editions First, an imprint of Edi8, 12 avenue d'Italie, 75013 Paris, France.

All notations of errors or omissions should be addressed to Thunder Bay Press, Editorial Department, at the above address.
All other correspondence (author inquiries, permissions) concerning the content of this book should be addressed to Édition First, an imprint of Édi8, Paris, France

Thunder Bay Press
Publisher: Peter Norton
Publishing Team: Lori Asbury, Ana Parker, Laura Vignale
Editorial Team: JoAnn Padgett, Melinda Allman, Dan Mansfield

ISBN: 978-1-62686-662-1

Printed in China

20 19 18 17 16   2 3 4 5 6

At the end you will find blank cards
for creating your own drawings
and calming messages!

COLOR YOURSELF CALM POSTCARDS

50 PEACEFUL PASSAGES TO COLOR AND SHARE

LISA MAGANO AND CHARLOTTE LEGRIS

THUNDER BAY
P · R · E · S · S
San Diego, California

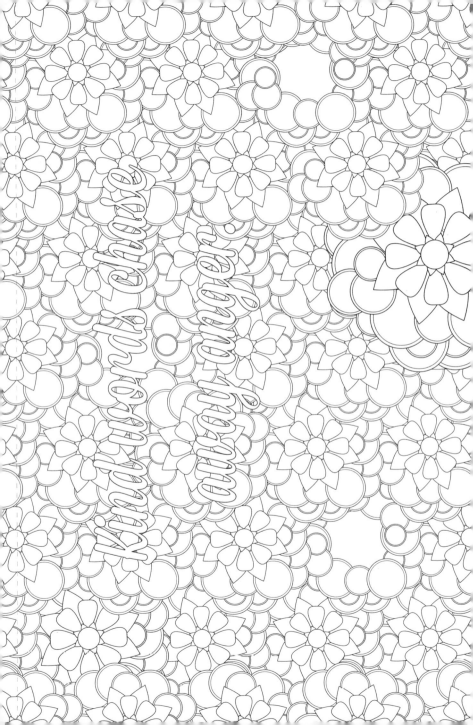

ADDITIONAL
POSTAGE
REQUIRED

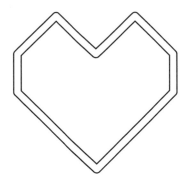

SILENCE WITH LOVED ONES IS NOT SILENCE.

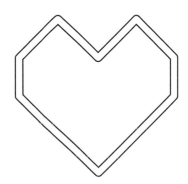

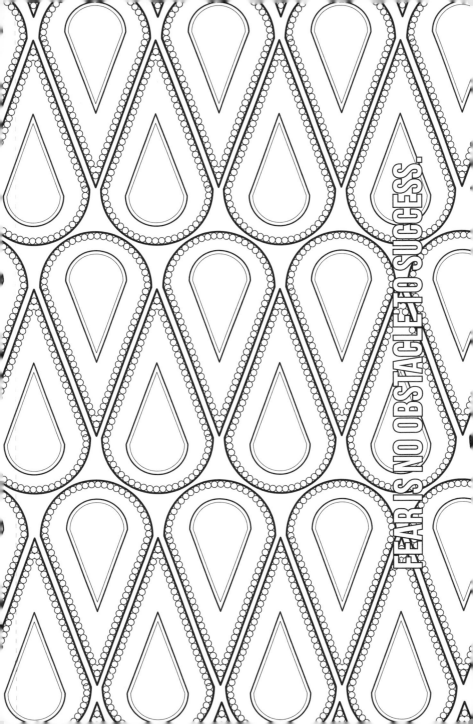

FEAR IS NO OBSTACLE TO SUCCESS.

ADDITIONAL
POSTAGE
REQUIRED

Re-create calmness each moment.

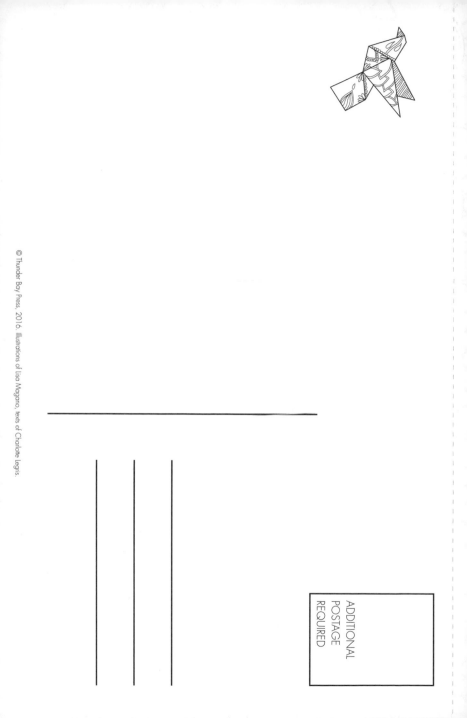

ADDITIONAL
POSTAGE
REQUIRED

My spirit is my own sanctuary, a haven of calmness.

I SEEK
INNER HARMONY.

To be strong, accept your weaknesses.

ADDITIONAL
POSTAGE
REQUIRED

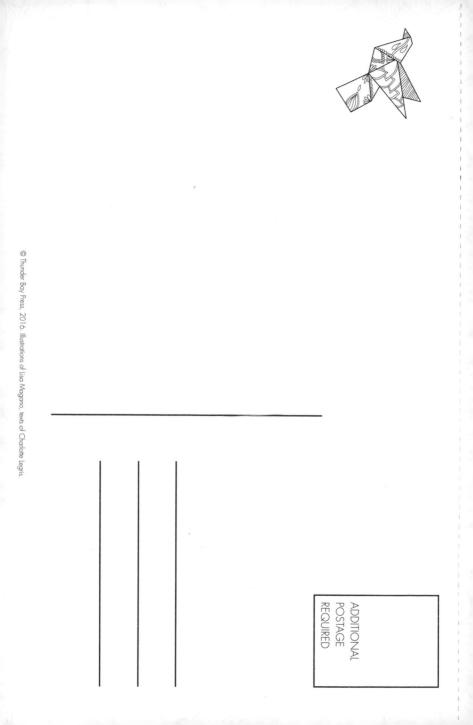

ADDITIONAL
POSTAGE
REQUIRED

ADDITIONAL
POSTAGE
REQUIRED

A moment of solitude is an opportunity.

ADDITIONAL
POSTAGE
REQUIRED

I PUT ASIDE THE REGRET THAT KEEPS ME FROM HAPPINESS.

The sun nourishes me.

I SEEK SILENCE IN MY SPIRIT.

ADDITIONAL
POSTAGE
REQUIRED

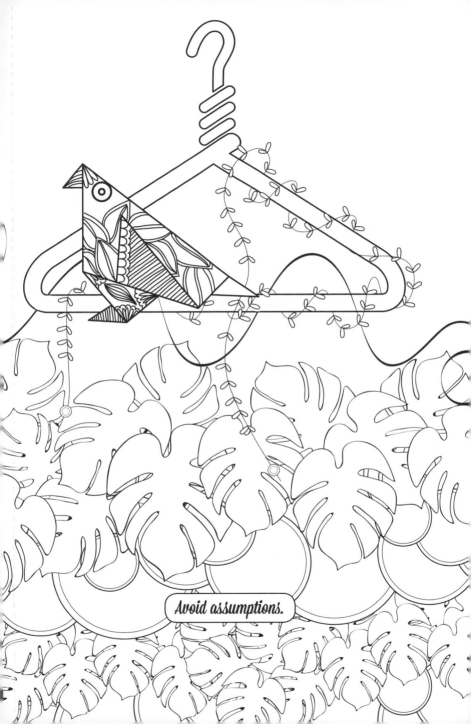

Avoid assumptions.

My center is my stability.

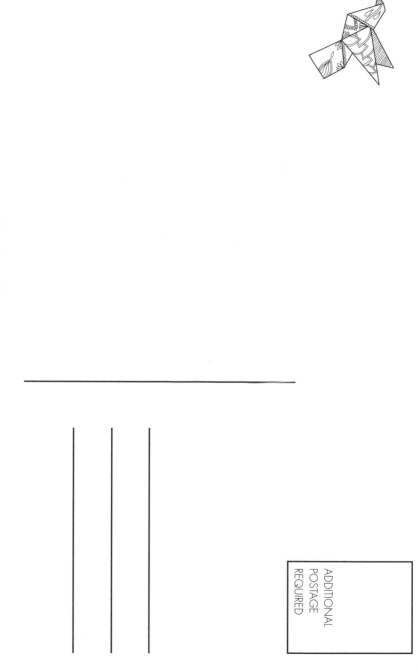

ADDITIONAL
POSTAGE
REQUIRED

DO
SOMETHING
DELIGHTFUL
EVERY DAY.

ADDITIONAL
POSTAGE
REQUIRED

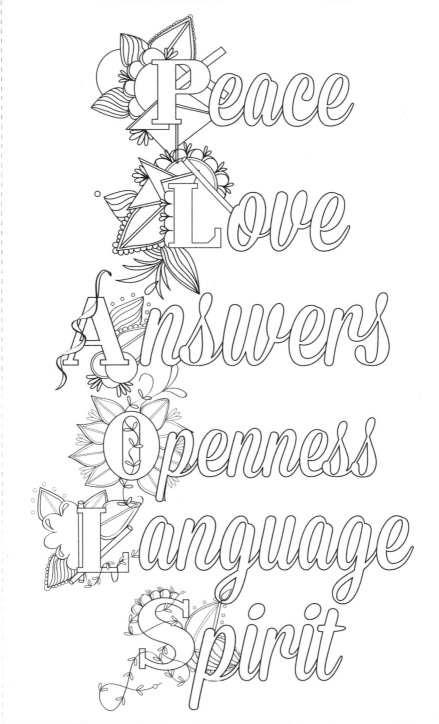

ADDITIONAL
POSTAGE
REQUIRED

ADDITIONAL
POSTAGE
REQUIRED

Today I have endless opportunities to receive.

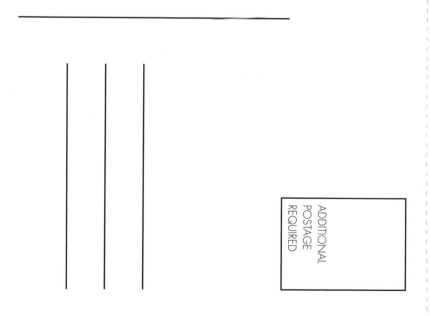

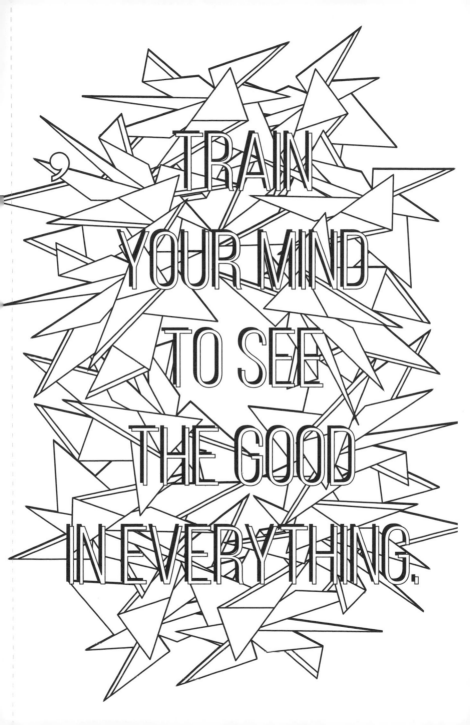

ADDITIONAL
POSTAGE
REQUIRED

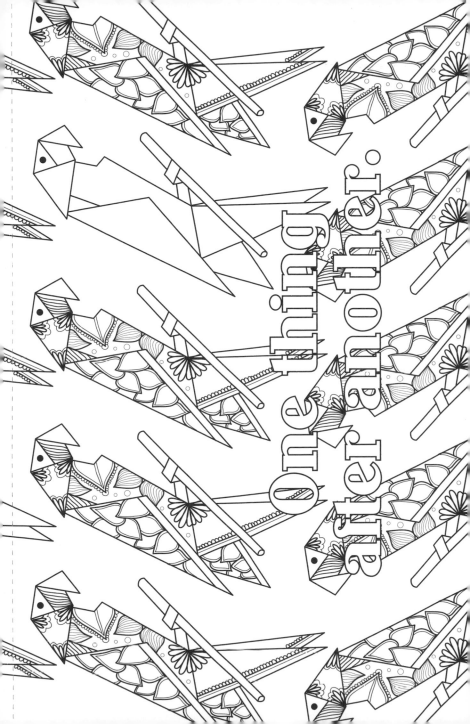

One thing after another.

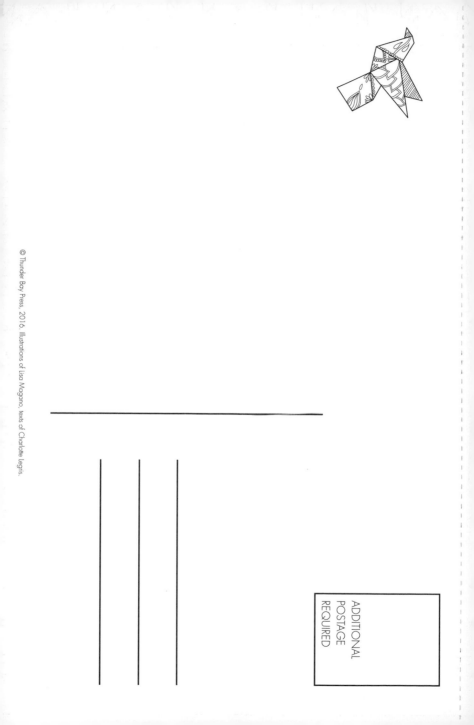

ADDITIONAL
POSTAGE
REQUIRED

Listen to the city at night.

ADDITIONAL
POSTAGE
REQUIRED

Inhale confidence and exhale all fears.

ADDITIONAL
POSTAGE
REQUIRED

TIME SOOTHES EVERY RAGE.

ADDITIONAL
POSTAGE
REQUIRED

ADDITIONAL
POSTAGE
REQUIRED

It's okay to ask for help.

ADDITIONAL
POSTAGE
REQUIRED

Happiness is a path.

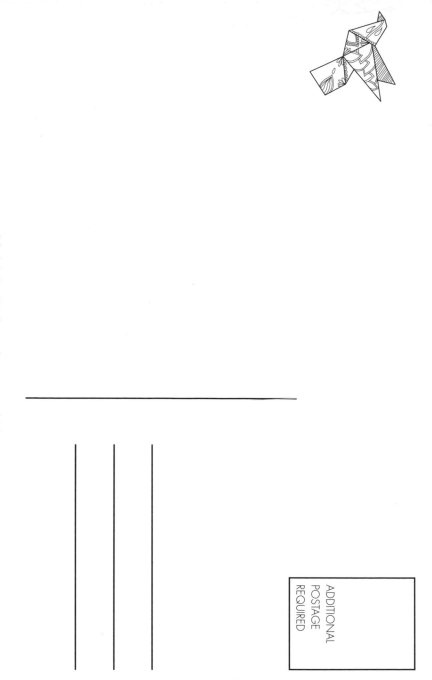

ADDITIONAL
POSTAGE
REQUIRED

Listen so you can speak. Speak so you can listen.

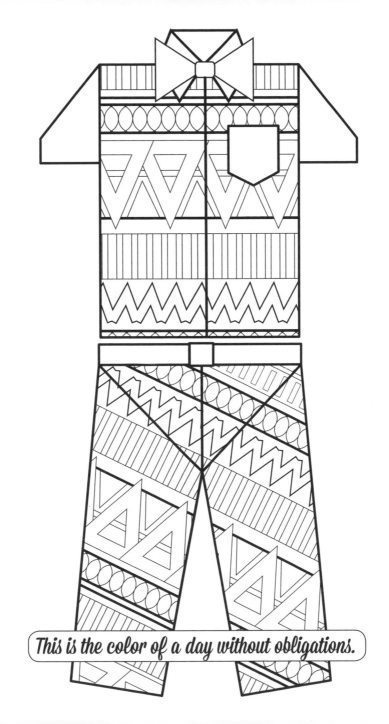

This is the color of a day without obligations.

ADDITIONAL
POSTAGE
REQUIRED

ADDITIONAL
POSTAGE
REQUIRED

I thank the talkers who teach me silence.

The past may shape you, but it does not define you.

ADDITIONAL
POSTAGE
REQUIRED

WORK IS REST FOR THE SPIRIT.

Give thanks every day.

ADDITIONAL
POSTAGE
REQUIRED

I LISTEN TO MY
WEARINESS'

ADDITIONAL
POSTAGE
REQUIRED

I KEEP SILENCE AND SILENCE KEEPS ME

ADDITIONAL
POSTAGE
REQUIRED

Meditation.

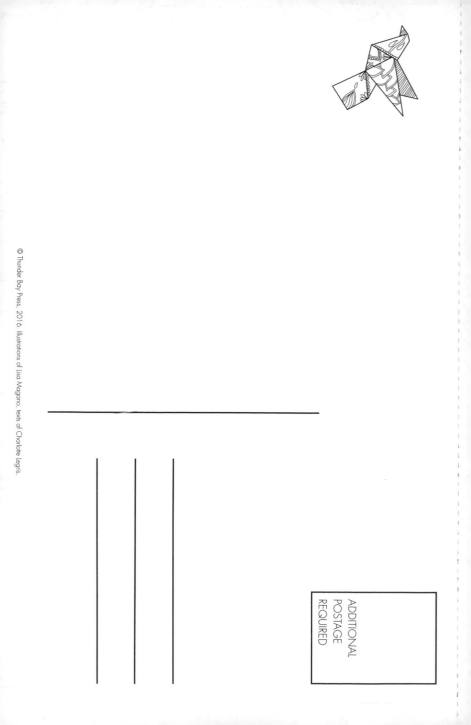

ADDITIONAL
POSTAGE
REQUIRED

I LISTEN TO
MY HEART BEAT.

Cherish what you have.

ADDITIONAL
POSTAGE
REQUIRED

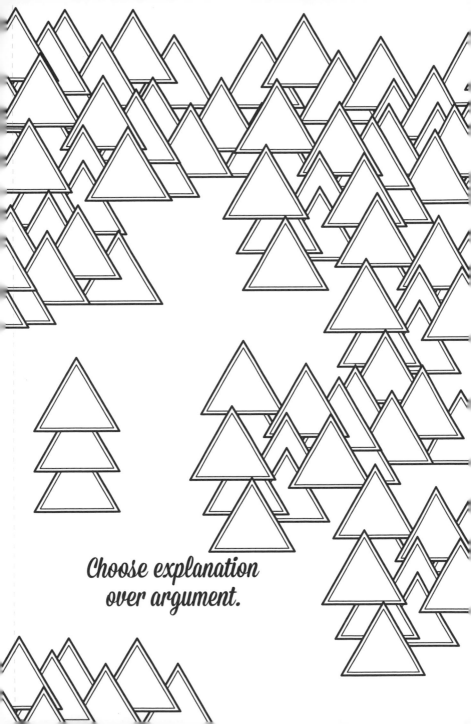

Choose explanation
over argument.

THE SPIRAL OF CALM.

DARING.

ADDITIONAL
POSTAGE
REQUIRED

Learn something every day.

ADDITIONAL
POSTAGE
REQUIRED

EVERY BREATH I TAKE
FILLS ME WITH HARMONY AND PEACE.

ADDITIONAL
POSTAGE
REQUIRED

ADDITIONAL
POSTAGE
REQUIRED